The Ultimate Tomato Container Gardening Guide for Beginners

How to Grow Homegrown Tomatoes in Small Spaces and Containers

Chloé Maëlle

Table of Contents

Introduction   *1*

Chapter 1: Choosing a Container   *3*

Chapter 2: Choosing a Tomato Variety   *7*

Chapter 3: Setting-Up the Container Garden   *11*

Chapter 4: Advantages and Disadvantages of Container Gardening   *17*

Chapter 5: Common Mistakes When Growing Tomatoes in Containers   *21*

Chapter 6: Final Thoughts and Tips   *23*

Conclusion   *27*

Preview of Next Book   *29*

Check Out My Other Books   *33*

One Last Thing…   *35*

Introduction

I want to thank you and congratulate you for purchasing this book!

This book contains proven steps and strategies on how to grow tomatoes in your very own container garden.

Having container gardens is a growing trend; millions of households are beginning to plant their own container gardens. It saves a lot of space, helps control pest problems, overcome soil issues, and most importantly, lets you enjoy homegrown produce fresh from your own container garden. Growing tomatoes in containers can be incredibly rewarding and satisfying.

Thanks again for purchasing this book, I hope you enjoy it! Please take some time to stop by and LIKE our Facebook page:

https://www.facebook.com/joypublishing

With gratitude,

Chloe Maëlle

Chapter 1: Choosing a Container

Choosing the right container is one of the most important things to do to make sure that the tomato-growing will be successful. A rule of thumb when choosing a container is to get a big enough container; the more space the root of the tomato plant has, the better the roots will grow, allowing for the top part of the plant to grow large. Generally, for one plant, you will need a container at that's at least a square foot or 2, but the one of the best you can get is a five gallon bucket which can be seen at hardware stores. Tomatoes can grow up to 6 to 8 feet tall and 2 feet across. Small containers can also be used to grow small plants, but that would also mean less fruit.

The minimum size of a pot for a patio tomato should be 14 inches in diameter and a capacity of at least 5 gallons. If you want to get the best results, find a pot that is 17 to 20 inches and can hold about 15 to 20 gallons.

If you are a beginner in gardening, you can succeed in growing tomatoes in containers when you select the suitable tomato variety for your container type.

Container Materials

Containers come in an assortment of materials, with each of them having a distinct advantage over the others.

- *Plastic*. Plastic containers are practical, inexpensive, and have become one of the most popular container choices. They can survive freezing and thawing, and can retain moisture. Soil in plastic pots requires less watering.

- *Wood.* Wood containers tend to be rot-resistant, especially those made of cypress, cedar, and redwood. It can provide great insulation, but may be more expensive than the plastic containers.

- *Terra Cotta.* These types of containers are good choices for they give good circulation to the plants, and water and air move well through them because of their natural material. They also have the ability to blend in well almost everywhere. However, the downside of terra cotta containers is that they dry out quickly. Tomatoes placed in these containers need to be monitored and made sure that they still have enough water. Another thing is that extreme temperature changes can make these containers crack easily, and may need replacing from time to time.

- The 3 types mentioned above are the most commonly used ones, but there are also others like concrete, cast iron, wire, pressed paper, metal, and fiberglass.

- Unconventional ideas for containers include rain barrels, milk cartons, egg cartons, 2 liter bottles, Styrofoam cups, and coffee cups. Most of these, though are for short term only.

Shape of Container

When choosing a container, keep in mind that square, cylindrical, or rectangular containers need less watering compared to pots that are tapered. There is more soil at the top of tapered pots, meaning it dries out more quickly. On the other hand, containers that are rectangular, cylindrical, or square have more volume of soil in the container's lower half and retain moisture better. Also, tomato plants grown in containers with straight sides tend to have healthier, more robust root systems.

Tomato Bags

Gardeners in England have, for years, made the most of what they can with very limited garden space by growing their tomatoes in bags of compost, topsoil, or potting soil. Grow bags make for instant gardens especially in areas where there are no minimal to no soil. An advantage of a grow bag is that the roots of the plant extend to the edge of the bag, then the plant sprouts newer roots elsewhere along the tap, meaning that the root system in grow bags are healthier and stronger. The disadvantage of a grow bag is that they dry out very quickly, meaning they have to be watered regularly. The best grow bags are made of double-layer polypropylene which are stronger and can last longer than the regular ones made of sheet plastic.

Other Tips

- It would be ideal to go with a light-colored container since they are less likely to absorb heat, and would likely keep the roots cool during the warm seasons.

- Put the heavy or oversized pots on a platform with wheels for them to be easily moved when the situation calls for it.

- When choosing a container, it is best to avoid those with narrow openings, or cheap plastic. Narrow openings would hinder a plant's full growing potential and cheap plastic would dry out with extended exposure to the sun.

- Make sure that the container that would be chosen would secure the weight of the plant when heavily loaded with plump, ripe fruits.

In the end, the size of the pot is more important than the material. As long as there is enough soil volume, tomatoes can grow well in terra cotta pots, ceramic pots, plastic pots, or deep wooden boxes. This does not mean, however, that the material does not play a part in your container gardening for they can make a difference. Materials like terra cotta and glazed ceramic can hold heat while lighter materials like wood or plastic can release heat more quickly.

Deciding on what container to get would depend on a lot of things. Size, shape, color, and material are all to be considered when picking a container. You would also have to keep in mind where you will be placing the container and choose the appropriate size to make sure it would suit the area you chose.

Chapter 2: Choosing a Tomato Variety

Tomatoes are very diverse plants that can come in all shapes and sizes. There is the dwarf variety which comes in under 2 feet, the determinate or bushing variety which are from 2 to 4 feet, and finally the indeterminate variety which are huge. The good thing is, any tomato, regardless of its size, can be grown in a container, as long as the container has room enough for the plant.

Dwarves are compact, which mean that you will not need a big container for them. The determinate kind can be sustained in a 12 inch deep pot, with the indeterminate kind needing at least a 16 inch deep container.

Certain characteristics can also come into play when picking a tomato fruit variety.

- *Resistance to Disease.* Some tomato varieties are more prone to certain diseases than others. It is advised to check if the plant is resistant to fusarium and verticillium, which are two of the most common diseases that can harm tomatoes.

- *Time it takes to Mature.* Each tomato plant has its own maturity time, or the time it takes for its fruit to ripen. It is important to know this in relation to the growing season.

- *Fruit Characteristics.* Some tomato fruits are more suitable for a particular use, such as for sandwiches, salads, and for direct eating. Knowing for what purpose the tomatoes would be used for is helpful in determining what variety to choose.

- *Growth Habit.* This is important to know because some tomato plants would need enough room for it to grow properly. This would also affect the type of container that would be used.

There is an assortment of tomatoes available, each bearing different types of fruit. The following are some tomatoes you can find:

> *Sungold.* These tomatoes are little, colored orange, and are sweet and plentiful. They are not hug, sprawling plants, and so they do well in containers.

> *Silver Fir Tree.* This variety of tomato plant has lots of ferns, has feathery, silvery gray-green foliage, and has round red fruits. The plants are compact and so they do well in small containers.

> *Black Seaman.* A wonderful black heirloom that does well in mid-sized containers and produces good-sized tomatoes.

> *Black Krim.* This plant produces large, attractive, purplish-red fruits which, as they ripen, turn violet-brown at the stem end. The flavor is also quite full and complex.

> *Green Sausage.* A plant that produces a lot of stripe, pretty, elongated fruits that are good for sauces and chutneys.

> *Golden Delight.* Mid-sized plant that produces yellow, low-acid fruit.

> *Cherokee Green.* These are medium sized tomatoes that are easy to grow, tasty and even look good. Its fruits are green and its blossom end turns yellowish-orange when ripe.

- *Stupice.* An ideal variety for those who live in areas with cool climates. The plants are compact and have potato-leaf foliage, while the fruits are red and about 2 inches in diameter. This variety also produces well all season.

- *Brandywine.* This variety is quite large, but regular pruning and some strong stakes, they can be maintained. The tomatoes are flavorful and are generally considered one of the best-tasting tomatoes.

- *Supersweet 100.* Each plant of Supersweet 100 can produce hundreds of bite-sized tomatoes. Its fruit is very sweet. It typically produces around 20 fruits, but when taken care of properly, may grow up to 100 fruits.

- *Big Beef.* Produces big fruits that can reach up to 6 inches in diameter.

- *Juliet.* Its fruit is oval and is hard, smooth, and dense. It takes about 60 days for it to mature.

There are a lot more tomato plant varieties available out there, and it is up to you to decide on which one you would want to plant in your container garden. Each kind of plant has their own look and feel, and also produces tomatoes with their own flavor and size. Many gardeners would recommend getting one of a bush type variety since they tend not to grow high.

Heirlooms

Heirloom tomato plants can grow in any pot as long as proper growing techniques are used. The best method to grow this type of tomato in pots is to begin with the determinate varieties. They grow up to 4 feet in height and trellising and staking need not be done for their care. Some heirloom plants include:

- *Principe Borghese.* One of the larger varieties that has a small egg-shaped fruit with a rich flavor.

- *Paul Robeson.* A tomato with a rich purple color and a strong, sweet flavor and a juicy, smooth texture.

- *Manitoba.* A slicer developed in Manitoba, Canada with a refreshing and tangy taste.

- *Green Zebra.* Very popular for its natural lemony flavor and its unique appearance.

- *New Yorker.* A Bush Beefsteak type that produces 4 to 6 fruits with a balanced flavor. These plants set well in cool growing conditions.

- *Riesentraube.* This type of tomato has its proverbial roots in Germany. Its name translates to "giant bunch of grapes." The plant produces huge groups of fruits, around 20-40. It can take up to 85 days for it to mature.

- *Japanese Black Triefele.* These plants are compact and the tomatoes it bears have a distinct smoky flavor and a gorgeous bronze color.

Hybrids

For a beginner gardener, hybrid plants are the best to start with. A hybrid means that one type of tomato was mixed with another type to create a new type of tomato. Hybrid plants have the advantage of "hybrid vigor" which means that they are often stronger and healthier. Most hybrid plants are also made specifically to produce bigger fruit. Some of the most common varieties of tomato hybrids include Early Girl, Beefmaster, and Better Boy.

Chapter 3: Setting-up the Container Garden

Once it has been decided what containers to get and what varieties of tomatoes to grow, it is time to set up the container garden. Before anything else, it is important to buy soil that is particularly for tomatoes or you can also make your own. Regular potting soil can be used to fill hanging planters and smaller pots however, for bigger pots or containers, a soil-less growing mix must be used. If you would chose to make your own, it is recommended to mix potting soil, peat moss, perlite, and compost in equal proportions. Compost is the one of the best for plants and it helps them to be cool and moist during the summer.

The first thing to do is to make sure the containers have drainage to keep the plants from drowning and from becoming soggy. The way to do this is by making drainage holes at the bottom of the container. This can be done by using a drill, or a hammer with a large nail. You can put as many holes as possible and the more holes the better. Once the holes are made, they must be covered in order to keep the soil from leaching out. Keep in mind that the holes must be covered enough to keep the soil in, and let water out. There are a couple of ways this can be achieved:

- *Plastic window screening.* This is a cheap and easy way to cover the drainage holes. Big plastic window screens are used and cut into pieces to fit into the bottom of the container.

- *Coco fiber, moss, or burlap.* These make for great pot liners especially for wire or hanging baskets.

- *Packing peanuts.* There are a lot of people who use packing peanuts in the bottom of their pots because they are inexpensive. The only thing is, they can stick everywhere inside the container if poured carelessly. It is a good idea to put some plastic window screens between the soil and the plants in order to prevent the two from mixing together.

When the containers have the drainage ready, it's time to plant the tomato plants in them. Before planting, be sure to wet the soil mix well. Afterwards, arrange the plants in the pot, add the soil around them, and gently pat it down around the plants. Once it has been planted, give it a mild liquid fertilizer.

Now, it's time to do what is perhaps the vital part: taking care of them. The plants won't grow by themselves, and would need regular monitoring and maintenance in order to ensure that they grow healthy and live long.

Watering

The key to a successful tomato planting is to give the plants a consistent amount of water. Tomatoes in containers must be watered often since their roots cannot extend and look for extra moisture unlike those that grow in gardens. This is most especially during the summertime. You need to water the soil, not the plants. The goal here is to keep the soil moist; too much water and the root of the plants will rot, and too little water would cause the plant to be weak. The best time of the day to water the plants would be during the morning, when the plants use water more efficiently, and would give them a chance to dry off before the night.

Also, watch out for excessive rainfall, and make sure the containers don't get waterlogged. It is best to take the containers to shelter during these periods.

Fertilizing

Aside from watering, it is equally important to fertilize the plants regularly. Most potting soil has no nutrients in them, so fertilizer will be needed. It is advised to start tomatoes off with a slow-release fertilizer. There are tomato specific fertilizers that can be bought, but any all-purpose, slow fertilizer will also do. Do not excessively fertilize the tomato plants because the fertilizer does not leach unlike how it would with in the garden. When the plants begin to flower, then it is time to start supplemental feeding every few weeks. An ideal fertilizer is one that would provide both the macro and micronutrient needs of the tomatoes.

Sunlight

Container tomatoes need at least 6 to 8 hours of sunlight a day in order for them to produce fruit well and have a good harvest. Balconies and porches are great places to achieve this, but if you choose to grow them indoors, they must be in a place where they can get maximum sunlight, even if it means moving it from window to window. Take note, however, that too much heat can be harmful to tomatoes. Containers can heat up quickly in the summertime, especially if the container is dark-colored. When this happens, the root of the plants will be too hot for them to be able to set tomatoes. They will still blossom, but the flowers will just fall off.

Staking

It is needed to stake or support plants such as tomatoes. Do not wait long before staking potted tomatoes. An ideal is to place 2 to 3 stakes or cages because bush varieties will need them to help in supporting their branches and heavy fruit sets. Add the stakes or cages when planting the container. Staking is optional, but is recommended.

Pruning

Pruned tomato plants will produce less fruit, but they will be larger in size. There are two methods used in pruning tomato plants and each has their own advantages. The first method is pruning the plant by pinching away the suckers, which are the shoots that grow between the stem and the leaf stalk and do not contain blossoms. If you decide to go with this method, it should be done once a week to keep the plant free of the suckers.

The second way of pruning is by not actually pruning them and to just let the plant grow wild. Plants that are not pruned will require less water and produce more fruit, the downside being that the fruit will be smaller and the plant would need greater space to grow.

Other Tips

- Garden bugs do the most damage when the plants are stressed or starting to wilt, so make sure that they are well watered. Pests like aphids can be removed with your hands or can be sprayed with a water sprayer. With larger infestations, a mix of equal parts water and liquid detergent in a spray bottle can do the trick. There are also commercial organic pest sprays that can be bought.

- Remove dead leaves to help control bugs.

- Place containers on small blocks up off the ground to improve drainage.

- Always have fresh soil from time to time and never reuse.

- Plant tomatoes deeply. This way, roots will develop from the stems that are under the ground and the tomatoes will be stronger and healthier.

- The best time to pick tomato fruits is when they are completely red.

When the plants have blossomed, they must be gently, but firmly, tapped so that the pollen will fall upon other blossoms.

Chapter 4: Advantages and Disadvantages of Container Gardening

There are several benefits from growing tomatoes in containers that may not be achieved with perfectly manicured yards or vast plots of plants. First off, it is a great way to start if one has not ever tried to garden; even an amateur can pull it off. The following are some of the advantages of container gardening:

- Container gardening is well-liked by gardeners who live in an area with restricted space or don't have the luxury of an outdoor garden. Even the smallest space can hold a container garden—a garden can be designed that will thrive no matter the space limitations—no matter if you live in a condo, in suburbia, on a farm, or in a high-rise apartment without a patio.

- Growing tomatoes in containers also means that they can be placed anywhere as long as they will receive their minimum of 8 hours of sunlight. This includes balconies, patios, and even by the window sills.

- Growing tomatoes in a container within the house allows for it to be grown all-year round because it can be constantly repositioned to areas where it would have favorable growing conditions.

- Plants in the garden are not easily moved around in case they are threatened with harsh weather or unwanted pests. However, with containers it is easy to move them away and keep them under cover or inside.

- Having a tomato container garden gives the luxury of having fresh produce without having the need to visit the market. Fresh tomatoes will be available right in the comforts of the home.

- Plants that are not suitable to grow in the soil in the garden can instead be grown in a container. This adds variety to the tomatoes that are being grown.

- No weeding is necessary because of its small surface area—weed seeds will unlikely find their way into the containers.

- With a container garden, the tomato plants can be better protected from insect invasion, weed invasion, bird attacks, or from frost. The plants which need heavy amounts of sunlight can easily be repositioned to follow the patches of the sun. Also, container tomatoes can free up valuable space in a garden, especially for people with limited outdoor space. There is also no weeding and the plants have less chances of getting soil-borne plant diseases.

- Plants that are grown in containers have a less chance of getting diseases compared to those in the garden.

- Keeping the plants well-fed is easier because they are kept in a small, confined area, meaning all the nutrients will be absorbed solely by the plant itself. Plants in the garden have other plants next to them that can share the nutrients.

- Soil in pots often warms up faster compared to soil in the ground, making it possible for an early harvest.

- Kids enjoy container gardening and is a good way to introduce the hobby to them.

- Containers can also have an aesthetic benefit; decorative and well-designed pots and urns can add value to the home or garden.

There are also some disadvantages to container gardening. First, the size of the growing space is limited to the size of the container, which makes it difficult to grow a large family. Container gardens also mean more frequent upkeep because the soil is limited to the size of the container, meaning that the moisture in the soil is, too. This is why the tomato plants have to be watered more often than normal. Frequent watering may, in turn, lead to potentially draining vital nutrients from the soil, so the plants have to also be fertilized more often.

Chapter 5: Common Mistakes When Growing Tomatoes in Containers

Growing tomatoes are relatively easy to do, but mistakes are not uncommon to have, especially for those who are only beginning to partake in this style of gardening, or those who do not have any garden experience at all. The following are common mistakes that are made and must be avoided:

- *Small Containers.* It is more advantageous to have a bigger container for there to be more soil to hold the water. More soil also means that there are more available nutrients for the tomato plants.

- *Too Little Water.* The amount a tomato plant would need when it comes to water would depend on a number of factors including: the size of the pot, the kind of potting soil being used, wind, heat, and humidity. Some plants would need watering at least once or twice day.

- *Too Much Water.* It is also important not to water the plants excessively and possibly drown them. The key thing to remember when watering is to keep the soil consistently moist. Also make sure that the container has adequate drainage. Be sure to check the soil's moisture before watering. This can be done by putting your finger into the soil up to the knuckle. If the soil on your fingertip feels dry, then that would be the time to water the plant.

- *Not Enough Sunlight.* Tomatoes love the sun and needs direct sunlight for 6 to 8 hours a day. Make sure that there are no objects blocking the sun and keeping sunlight away from the plants.

- *Starving the Plants.* Tomatoes need to be heavily fed and fertilized. Potting mixes cannot be relied on to give the plants the nutrients it needs; most of the time, potting mixes have insufficient amounts of the required nutrients. Also, the nutrients can be quickly used up by the plants or just washed out with repeated watering.

- *Staking or Caging Too Late.* It is advised to set up the stakes or cages before the tomatoes grow big.

- *Plant to Pot Ratio.* Remember to keep in mind the proportion of the plant to the container it is going into. For example, don't place short plants into large containers. A plant must be at least as tall as its container.

- *Putting the Tomato Plant Outdoors Too Early.* You should wait for warm overnight temperatures before putting your tomato plants out. Take your plants outdoors during the daytime and back indoors at night. You may also leave it indoors as long as it gets enough sunlight through the windows.

- *No Fences around the Container Garden.* All sorts of animals can take an interest in your plants, so make sure to put barriers or fences around an outdoor container garden.

Chapter 6: Final Thoughts and Tips

Tomato container gardening can be a nice endeavor if you want to start a garden that is convenient. It can also be done no matter where you live. Having tomatoes in containers also means that their produce can be within arm's reach whenever you'll be needing them. It also saves you a lot of space in your home, especially if you do not have a dedicated area for your container garden. The containers can also aesthetically pleasing, since there are containers that have great designs and not just the plain, boring, pots.

One of the concerns when dealing with container gardening is rain. Unlike in non-container gardens where the rain water is distributed among the plants, rain water can fill containers very quickly and drown the plants. Other than that, container gardening can be easy if you do the right things to properly take care of the plants and avoid the common mistakes made by other container gardeners. If done correctly, you will have an assortment of tomatoes readily available when need or want them.

Ultimately, it is absolutely delightful to be able to grow your own tomatoes. You can enjoy fresh, organic tomatoes that taste good without needing a trip to the market.

Other Tips

- Remember that plants in containers require more frequent watering and fertilizing.

- The soil in the container need to be at least 24 inches deep, and must be changed every two years.

- It is advised to start off with transplants instead of seeds. Also look for the compact varieties of tomatoes.

- Cherry and pear tomatoes are perfect for instant eating.

- Fish or seaweed emulsion is good fertilizer for containers.

- It is recommended to feed liquid fertilizer to the tomato plants at least once a week.

- It is not only the big plants that need a big container, but also the plants that take long to mature.

- If the tomato containers are on the rooftops, make sure there is a setup that would resist strong winds, since it can get very windy up there.

- Look for a potting mix that is made up of organic matter. At least one of the ingredients should be compost, bark fines, or peat. Potting mixes with organic matter will absorb lots of water and will, in turn, give the roots of the plants with the needed aeration.

- Make sure to freshen up the soil every year. This can be done by removing the top few inches of the soil and then adding some new soil in, then fertilizing it.

- If the plant you got is root bound, some roots may have to be cut out in order for it to slide out of its nursery pot. In cases where it is still difficult to get the plant out, the nursery pot would have to be broken. Remember to never pull the plant out by its stem, or it can die before the garden can even be started.

Identifying Plant Problems

- *Hornworms.* These pests can cause big problems to a tomato plant by consuming the stems, leaves, and even the fruit, and then continues on to another plant. Hornworms are easy to miss even though they are big because they blend in with their green color. The simplest solution to hornworms is by plucking them out manually. An alternative would be to buy a Bacillus thuringiensis spray which is excellent at eliminating hornworms.

- *Blight.* This is a fungal infection that is seen as small, black lesions. These appear on the plant's foliage and stems, and will eventually appear on the fruit. The only way to save the plant is to cut off the affected limb. Most of the time, though, the affected plant is as good as gone.

- *Tomato Rot.* One of the most common problems when it comes to tomatoes. This is caused by a calcium deficiency, and can be prevented by making sure the container garden is enriched with organic compost.

- *Wilting.* One of the most serious problems for a tomato plant and its owner. Causes of wilting include lack of water, excessive water, or an infection. Remember that a tomato plant needs about an inch of water every week.

- *Septoria Leaf Spot.* This is a disease which comes in the form of brown spots that appear usually on the foliage that is nearer to the ground. This can be prevented through weeding, and proper fertilizing. It is also recommended to rotate the planting site every year.

Conclusion

Thank you again for purchasing my book.

I hope this book was able to help you to know more about tomato container gardening.

The next step is to go out and start buying containers, tomato plants or seedlings, fertilizer, soil, and you'll be ready to start your own container garden.

In addition, please remember to check out our Facebook page in order to find other resources and upcoming promotions:

https://www.facebook.com/joypublishing

With sincere thanks,

Chloé Maëlle

Preview Of "Vegetable Container Gardening Guide for Beginners: How to Grow Healthy Vegetable and Herb Gardens in Small Spaces and Containers"

Chapter 1: Planning your Container Garden

Congratulations on wanting to become self-sufficient! Growing your own food at home is a highly rewarding and healthy experience for you and your family. You will not only have access to the freshest and most delicious produce around, but also free your family and yourself from the harmful chemicals that often lace commercially produced vegetables and herbs.

Now, you chose this book for a specific reason, and that is to grow your own vegetables and herbs in containers. It is therefore safe to assume that you have limited amount of space and want to use organic or at least minimize the use of harmful chemicals. Also, the purpose of your container garden is probably for your family's personal consumption, which means that you might want to minimize cost.

It is indeed very excited to start planting, but do know that it is important to plan every last detail first to ensure that your plants will grow optimally and give you a bountiful harvest as much as a container garden can provide. So, without further ado, let us immediately get into planning your vegetable and herb container garden.

Choosing your Containers

The ideal container for growing vegetables in particular should be deep enough to allow your plants to develop a strong root system. Also, the container should have a minimum diameter of 24 inches.

You can either buy new containers or you can use existing ones that are lying around your home. Terra-cotta containers are generally considered good choices, but you can also re-use your old plastic trash bins by creating drainage holes in the base to turn them into pots. To maximize space, you can also consider using hanging containers.

Attractive-looking containers are very inspiring and motivating, which is why you might like to consider using glazed ceramic planters. The great thing about them is that the material is porous, which will allow the roots of your plants to have access to air. If this sounds too fancy, you can substitute with a polypropylene pot.

Each type of container has its pros and cons. For instance, clay or terra-cotta can break easily, especially by frost. Avoid using them if you live in the northern areas.

Cast concrete is very durable, except they are also very heavy and unsuitable for decks or balconies. Metal containers are durable as well, but they are heat conductors, which can damage your plants' roots. If you choose to use them, line them with plastic first.

Plastic and fiberglass containers are also sturdy and cheap, but make sure not to choose thin ones as these will become brittle and would eventually break.

Wooden containers look great and can protect the roots of your plants from fluctuating temperature changes. Pick only the rot-resistant variety such as locust, cedar or pine treated with a nontoxic preservative.

Planning your Garden Space

The size and number of containers that you need will depend upon the amount of space that you have available for your container garden. The important thing is that the space should have access to at least 6 hours of direct sunlight everyday (or 4 hours, depending on which plants you choose to grow). Ideally, your garden should be at a vicinity which you pass by every day, so that you won't accidentally neglect your plants. A water source should also be close by.

If you can, find a 24-inch container which can serve as your all-around container garden. This size can fit a large vegetable plant such as a tomato, eggplant or pepper, as well as allow you to grow tall plants such as okra or fennel. The extra space around the edges can be used for planting smaller herbs or greens such as lettuce or spinach.

If you have the tiniest bit of space available, you might want to consider a themed garden, such as planting vegetables and herbs that you use to create specific types of dishes. For instance, you can create an Italian cuisine vegetable and herb garden.

For those of you whose available garden space gets only 4 hours of direct sunlight, your best option would be to grow a salad garden full of leafy vegetables such as a lettuce, Swiss chard, and spinach. Root crops such as carrots, beets and radishes, will also fare well in this set-up. Just keep in mind that this type of garden will require a lot of organic compost and, eventually, more constant watering.

Now that you have gathered your containers and assessed your garden space, you can now move forward to another fun part of the planning, and that is to choose the vegetables and herbs that you can grow.

Check out the rest of this book on Amazon

Or go to: http://amzn.to/1p0DSEX

Check Out My Other Books

Below you'll find some of my other books that are popular on Amazon and Kindle as well. You can visit my author page on Amazon to see other work done by me. Alternatively, you can simply search for these titles on the Amazon website to find them.

Tomato Container Gardening Guide for Beginners: How to Grow Healthy Home Grown Tomatoes in Small Spaces and Containers

Vegetable Container Gardening Guide for Beginners: How to Grow Healthy Vegetable and Herb Gardens in Small Spaces and Containers

One Last Thing...

Source: Wikipedia

If you believe that this book is worth sharing, would you please take the time to let others know how it affected your life? If it turns out to make a difference in the lives of others, they will be forever grateful to you, as will I.

Made in the USA
Coppell, TX
01 February 2020

ISBN 9781502816412

90000

9 781502 816412